TOP SCORE
SPORTS STARS AND STATS

SLAM DUNK!

Mark Woods and Ruth Owen

Consultant Sally Smith

Evans

First published in 2010
by Evans Brothers Limited
2A Portman Mansions
Chiltern Street
London W1U 6NR
UK

Printed in China by New Era Co. Ltd

British Library Cataloguing in Publication Data
Woods, Mark.
      Slam dunk!. -- (Top score)
      1. Mathematics--Juvenile literature. 2. Mathematics--
      Problems, exercises, etc.--Juvenile literature.
      3. Basketball--Juvenile literature.
      I. Title II. Series III. Owen, Ruth, 1967-
      510-dc22
      ISBN-13: 9780237542788

VISIT OUR WEBSITE
Evans
www.evansbooks.co.uk

Developed & Created by Ruby Tuesday Books Ltd

Project Director – Ruth Owen
Designer – Alix Wood
Editor – Ben Hubbard
Consultants – Sally Smith, Hilary Koll and Steve Mills
© Ruby Tuesday Books Limited 2010

ACKNOWLEDGEMENTS

With thanks to the Year 5 and Year 6 students at St Cleer School, Liskeard, Cornwall for their invaluable feedback and help with the development of these books.

Images: Getty **7 right** (Noah Graham), **10 left** (Bruce Bennett Studios), **10 right** (Ted Mathias), **11** (Jerry Wachter), **12 top left** (De Paul/Collegiate Images), **12 top right**, **13 top** (Andrew D. Bernstein), **13 bottom** (Manny Millan), **14** (Andrew D. Bernstein), **15** (Mike Powell), **16-17** (Filippo Monteforte), **18** (Antonio Scorza), **20-21** (Barry Gossage), **24-25** (Doug Pensinger), **26** (Evan Gole). Shutterstock **front cover**, **title page**, **8**, **28 top**. Wikipedia (public domain) **7 left**, **12 bottom**, **22**, **28 bottom**, **29**.

While every effort has been made to secure permission to use copyright material, the publishers apologise for any errors or omissions in the above list and would be grateful for notification of any corrections to be included in subsequent editions.

MARK WOODS

Mark Woods is a sports journalist and regular BBC presenter and commentator. He writes on a variety of sports including football, basketball and rugby.

RUTH OWEN

Ruth Owen is a children's non-fiction writer who has developed a number of innovative maths practice books.

SALLY SMITH

Sally Smith has taught in primary, secondary and special schools and is currently a Leading Teacher for Maths. She has worked as a maths consultant for the Cornwall local authority.

CONTENTS

IT'S ALL ABOUT THE NUMBERS!

56

Basketball is all about numbers. What number is on the jersey of your favourite player? What height is he or she? How many points did a player score? Numbers help us play, coach and understand basketball.

12

89

2

41

Basketball was invented in 1891 by a Canadian teacher named James Naismith. He invented the indoor game to help his students keep fit in the winter. The sport soon became popular.

Basketball spread around the world and players began to play professionally (for money). Soon leagues, such as the NBA (National Basketball Association), were set up. The basic idea of the game is still the same, though – the side with the most points wins!

Being good at basketball takes practice. It's the same with numbers. When you practise your maths skills, you improve your maths fitness.

In January 2006, Kobe Bryant of the Los Angeles Lakers scored an amazing 81 points in a game against the Toronto Raptors.

63

James Naismith used a football and two peach baskets for the first ever game of basketball.

Kobe Bryant

JUMP SHOT

A jump shot is when you jump to get power and height while shooting.

Let's get started!

BASKETBALL BASICS

Basketball is a team sport. It helps to have a superstar player, but it takes five players and a coach working together to win a game.

The hoop is 3.05 metres above the ground.

In most leagues, each team must shoot within 24 seconds of getting the ball. If the team runs out of time, they lose possession of the ball. The shot clock counts down the 24 seconds.

GAME ON

- A game lasts for 40 or 48 minutes.
- A game is divided into two halves or four quarters.
- If the score is tied at the end of a game, an extra period is played.

SCORING POINTS

Players try to put the ball through the hoop to win points.
- **1 point** – from a free throw given after a team commits a foul.
- **2 points (Field Goal)** – awarded for a shot taken within the D-shaped arc close to the basket.
- **3 points** – awarded for a long range basket taken from outside the D-shaped arc.

A FOUL

A foul is when a player does something against the rules. A player can only foul five or six times; after that he or she is out of the game.

28 m

15 m

Basketball court

BASKETBALL BASICS QUIZ

Get started with these basketball basics quiz questions.

1) If a 48-minute basketball game is played in four quarters, how long will each quarter last?

2) Look at these shot clocks. If each clock started at 24 seconds, how many seconds have passed?

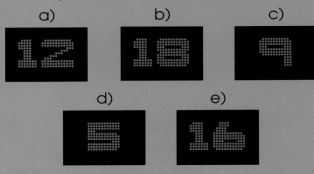

a) 12   b) 18   c) 9

d) 5   e) 16

3) The shot clock starts at 24 seconds. Clare takes 5 seconds to pass to Jo. Then Jo takes 3 seconds to pass to Ellie. Ellie dribbles the ball for 7 seconds, then she passes to Sue. Sue tries to make a shot but gets blocked for 4 seconds. How many seconds are left on the shot clock?

4) Look at the basketball court picture. What is the perimeter of the court?

5) A player is 1.91 metres tall. What is the distance from the top of the player's head to the hoop?

RECORD BREAKERS

In 1962, Wilt Chamberlain of the Philadelphia Warriors scored 100 points in an NBA game against the New York Knicks. In 1983, the highest-scoring game of all time was won by the Detroit Pistons. They beat the Denver Nuggets 186–184. Breaking records is all about numbers!

TALLEST BASKETBALL PLAYERS

Suleiman Ali Nashnush	Libya	2.45 m
Sung Mingming	China	2.36 m
Gheorghe Muresan	Romania	2.31 m
Manute Bol	Sudan	2.31 m
Margo Dydek	Poland	2.18 m

Wilt Chamberlain (Philadelphia Warriors) grabs a rebound in a game against the Detroit Pistons in 1961. He once grabbed a record-breaking 55 rebounds in a game against the Boston Celtics!

REBOUND

A rebound is when you catch the ball after a missed shot.

Michael Jordan tries to get around Gheorghe Muresan.

10

Manute Bol and teammate Tyrone "Muggsy" Bogues of the Baltimore Bullets were the tallest and shortest players in the NBA in 1987.

Use the record-breaking statistics and facts to answer these quiz questions.

1) Look at the **Tallest Basketball Players** box. Which player is closest in height to 240 cm?

2) What is the difference in height between Tyrone "Muggsy" Bogues and Manute Bol? Give your answer in centimetres.

3) Look at these heights of a basketball team. Put the heights in order from shortest to tallest.

   2.01 m   2.30 m   1.89 m   2.10 m   1.98 m

4) In the 1953 Eurobasket Championship, the Soviet Union beat Denmark 118–14. It was the biggest ever difference in scores in an international game. What was the difference?

5) In December 1991, the Cleveland Cavaliers beat the Miami Heat 148–80. It was the biggest ever difference in an NBA game. What was the difference?

The shortest player to play in the NBA was Tyrone "Muggsy" Bogues. He was 1.6 metres tall.

11

BLAST FROM THE PAST

Some players have left their mark on basketball history!

George Mikan was known as "Mr. Basketball". He was famous for wearing glasses when he played.

99

1950s – GEORGE MIKAN

Games: 439
Points: 10,156
Assists: 1245
Field goals made: 3544
NBA All Star Games: 4

Kareem Abdul-Jabbar used his deadly "skyhook" shot to overcome tall opponents.

33

1970s – KAREEM ABDUL-JABBAR

Games: 1560
Points: 38,387
Rebounds: 17,440
Assists: 5660
Field goals made: 15,837
NBA All Star Games: 18

AN ASSIST

An assist is a pass that leads to a basket being scored.

6

1960s – BILL RUSSELL

Games: 963
Points: 14,522
Rebounds: 21,620
Assists: 4100
Field goals made: 5687
NBA All Star Games: 12
Olympic gold medalist: 1956

Bill Russell (left) played for and coached the Boston Celtics from 1956 to 1969. The team won 11 NBA championships – a record!

Earvin "Magic" Johnson was one of the most popular players ever and helped to make the NBA an important sports league across the world.

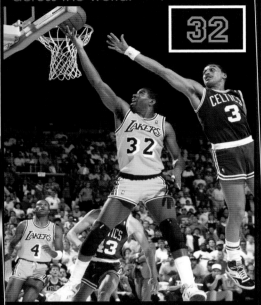

32

1980s – MAGIC JOHNSON

Games: 906
Points: 17,707
Rebounds: 6559
Assists: 10,141
Field goals made: 6211
NBA All Star Games: 11
Olympic gold medalist: 1992

BASKETBALL HISTORY QUIZ

Use the players' facts and statistics to answer these quiz questions.

1) Which player had –
   a) The most rebounds?
   b) The most assists?
   c) The second highest number of points?

2) Look at the large numbers below. What are the digits **in bold** worth?
   a) Michael Jordan points 32,2**9**2
   b) George Mikan assists 1**2**45
   c) Bill Russell rebounds 2**1**,620

3) Round each player's number of games to the nearest hundred.

4) Do this calculation which uses the players' jersey numbers.
   99 + 6 + 33 – 32 – 23 =

5) Which player played more games than Bill Russell, but fewer games than Kareem Abdul-Jabbar?

23

1990s – MICHAEL JORDAN

Games: 1072
Points: 32,292
Rebounds: 6672
Assists: 5633
Field goals made: 12,192
NBA All Star Games: 13
Olympic gold medalist: 1984, 1992

Most basketball fans agree that Michael "Air" Jordan is the greatest ever player because of his ability to score and defend.

THE DREAM TEAM

The USA men's team at the 1992 Olympic Games in Spain may be the greatest line-up basketball has ever seen. It was the first time that professional NBA players were allowed to play for their country's side. The team won every game to win the gold medal. The 1992 USA squad became known as "The Dream Team".

THE DREAM TEAM

Guards
Magic Johnson
Michael Jordan
John Stockton
Clyde Drexler

Forwards
Larry Bird
Scottie Pippen
Karl Malone
Chris Mullin
Christian Laettner
Charles Barkley

Centres
David Robinson
Patrick Ewing

The Dream Team with their coach Chuck Daly.

A basketball team has 10 or 12 players. Five are on court at any one time. The best five players are normally "the starting 5".

14

Drazen Petrovic of Croatia lays the ball up over Scottie Pippen of the USA in the 1992 Olympic final.

DREAM TEAM QUIZ

Use the Dream Team's statistics to answer these questions.

1) Look at the **Dream Team Results** table. What was the difference in scores for each game?

2) What was the biggest difference in scores? What was the smallest?

3) Below are the US team's scores. Round each score to the nearest ten.
   a) **116**   b) **127**   c) **103**   d) **122**
   e) **111**   f) **115**   g) **127**   h) **117**

4) Add up the USA team's scores for the eight games. Now use a calculator to find the USA team's mean score.

5) Look at the gold medals. What fraction of each medal has been shaded in red?

DREAM TEAM RESULTS

Group stage
USA 116–48 Angola
USA 127–83 Brazil
USA 103–70 Croatia
USA 122–81 Spain
USA 111–68 Germany

Quarter finals
USA 115–77 Puerto Rico

Semi finals
USA 127-76 Lithuania

Final
USA 117-85 Croatia

a)   b)   c)

d)   e)

2008 USA OLYMPIC TEAM

At the 2008 Olympic Games in China, the USA men's basketball team was once again made up of top NBA stars. And once again, the team won all their games to take gold.

2008 USA OLYMPIC TEAM

Guards
Jason Kidd
Kobe Bryant
Chris Paul
Dwyane Wade
Michael Redd
Deron Williams

Forwards
Carmelo Anthony
LeBron James
Carlos Boozer
Tayshaun Prince

Centres
Chris Bosh
Dwight Howard

2008 TEAM RESULTS

Group stage
USA 101–70 China
USA 97–76 Angola
USA 92–69 Greece
USA 119–82 Spain
USA 106–57 Germany

Quarter finals
USA 116–85 Australia

Semi finals
USA 101–81 Argentina

Final
USA 118–107 Spain

Kobe Bryant of the USA goes for a slam dunk against Argentina in the semi finals.

2008 USA OLYMPIC TEAM QUIZ

Use the 2008 team's statistics to answer these quiz questions.

1) Look at the USA team's eight sets of points in the **2008 Team Results** table. Which numbers are odd numbers and which are even?

2) Use the **2008 Team Results** table to answer these questions.
   a) Which team did the USA beat by 49 points?
   b) Which teams did the USA beat by 31 points?
   c) Which was the closest game in the whole competition?

3) Now do these calculations. The answers match the USA team's scores.
   a) **10 x 11 + 8**
   b) **150 − 31**
   c) **32 + 22 + 10 + 33**
   d) **32 ÷ 2 + 100**

4) How many points had the USA team won by the end of the group stage?

5) Add up all the USA team's points to find their competition total. Now do the same for the 1992 Dream Team (on pages 14-15). Which of the two great USA teams earned the most points?

WORLD CHAMPIONS

Teams from all over the world take part in the FIBA World Championships. To be a world champion is an even bigger honour for many basketball players than winning an Olympic gold medal. There is a women's and a men's World Championship competition.

Lauren Jackson of Australia tries to score against France in the 2006 World Championship.

MEN'S WORLD CHAMPIONSHIPS

Countries take it in turn to host the competition.

Year	Host country
1970	Yugoslavia
1974	Puerto Rico
1978	Philippines
1982	Colombia
1986	Spain
1990	Argentina
1994	Canada
1998	Greece
2002	USA
2006	Japan
2010	Turkey

MEDALS PICTOGRAM
WOMEN'S WORLD CHAMPIONSHIPS

This pictogram shows the medals table from 1979 to 2006.

USA	
Korea	
Canada	
Soviet Union/ Russia	
China	
Yugoslavia	
Cuba	
Brazil	
Australia	

KEY Gold   Silver   Bronze

WORLD CHAMPIONS QUIZ

Try these World Championships quiz questions.

1) Look at the **Men's World Championships** table.
   a) How often is the competition held?
   b) In what years will the next two competitions be held?

2) Look at this sequence of years. Can you fill in the missing years?
   1980   1982   1985   ?   1994   ?   2007

3) Which country hosted the Men's World Championship 20 years after Spain?

4) Look at the **Medals Pictogram**.
   a) Which countries have won two bronze medals?
   b) How many gold medals has the USA won?

5) Draw this Venn diagram. Now add the women's teams in the correct place within the diagram according to the medals they've won. We've added three teams to get you started.

BASKETBALL LEAGUES

Almost every country has a national basketball league. In North America, the biggest leagues are the NBA (National Basketball Association) and the WNBA (Women's National Basketball Association). Top basketball clubs in Europe compete in the Euroleague.

Tammy Sutton-Brown of the Indiana Fever battles for the tip-off against the Phoenix Mercury during the 2009 WNBA Finals.

TIP-OFF

A tip-off is when the ball is thrown up in the air between two players at the start of a game. This is done to decide which team starts off with the ball.

BIG LEAGUES QUIZ

Try answering these quiz questions about leagues.

1) Some leagues, such as the NBA and WNBA, use percentages to work out who wins the league. Look at the NBA league table below. The symbol % means percentage. Can you fill in the missing percentages?

	Games played	Games won	Games lost	% won
LA Lakers	50	25	25	?
Phoenix	64	16	48	25%
Golden State	80	72	8	?
LA Clippers	70	42	28	60%
Sacramento	50	20	30	40%

2) Write the five teams' percentages as decimals.

3) Now write the five teams' percentages as fractions.

4) Write your answers to question 3 in order, starting with the smallest.

5) Some leagues use a points system. If a team gets **3 points** for a win and **no points** if they lose, work out which numbers fill the gaps in this table.

	Games played	Games won	Games lost	Points
TEAM A	33	10	23	30
TEAM B	18	8	10	?
TEAM C	?	22	15	66
TEAM D	41	?	12	87
TEAM E	27	17	?	?

THE COACH

The coach's job is to decide on the team's tactics and work out the best way to beat the opposing team. The coach must also get the team ready for the game in practice and manage how they work together during a game.

The Los Angeles Lakers huddle around head coach Phil Jackson.

- The best five players normally start the game. They will get too tired, though, if they play the whole game. So, it's the coach's job to decide when to send on a reserve player.

- The coach can decide if the team plays fast or slow. It can take less than eight seconds to go from one end of the court and score, or up to 24 seconds.

- The coach can decide if the team shoots close to the basket or from long range.

WHO'S ON COURT?

Carl	Plays for 35 minutes
Dwight	Plays for 3/4 of the game
John	Joins the game in the 26th minute
Dean	On court for 32 minutes
Todd	Plays for 12 minutes

SHOOTING PRACTICE

a)

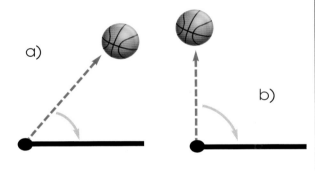

b)

c)

d)

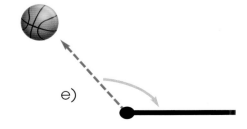

e)

YOU'RE THE COACH QUIZ

Try these quiz questions about team tactics.

1) Look at the **Who's On Court?** chart. If a game lasts 40 minutes –
   a) Which player will be substituted for five minutes?
   b) What fraction of the game does Dean play?
   c) How many minutes is Dwight on court?
   d) John comes on court and plays to the end. How many minutes is he on court?

2) Two reserves come on court after Todd. They play half of the remaining time each. For how many minutes is each reserve on court?

3) A team needs to score 36 points. Which of the shooting combos below will win the game?

   • **Free throw = 1 point**   • **Field goal = 2 points**
   • **Distance shot = 3 points**

   a) 10 x distance shots + 3 free throws
   b) 20 x free throws + 3 distance shots
   c) 27 x free throws + 3 distance shots

Look at the **Shooting Practice** pictures. Each shot is also an angle.

4) a) Which angle is 90°? What is this type of angle called?
   b) Which angle is 180°?

5) a) Which angle is obtuse?
   b) Which two angles are acute?

LEBRON VS MELO

To compare teams and players we use statistics. These numbers are worked out as average figures per game for different tasks. For example, Artis Gilmore of the Chicago Bulls made 59.9 percent (%) of his shots in his career – an NBA record! Here, we will compare the statistics of NBA stars LeBron James and Carmelo Anthony.

CARMELO ANTHONY

Carmelo Anthony grew up in the city of Baltimore in the USA. He set up a youth centre in the city that helps kids with education and life skills.

NBA team: Denver Nuggets
Position: Forward
Date of birth: 29th May, 1984
Height: 2.03 m

KEY TO STATISTICS

G: Games played
GS: Games started
MPG: Minutes per game
FG%: Field goal percentage
3P%: 3-point shots percentage
FT%: Free throw percentage
RPG: Rebounds per game
APG: Assists per game
SPG: Steals per game
BPG: Blocks per game
PPG: Points per game

COMPARE THE NBA STARS QUIZ

Now try these quiz questions.

The yellow table below shows LeBron James' and Carmelo Anthony's statistics. Use the **Key To Statistics** box to find out what the numbers mean.

NBA CAREER STATISTICS TO THE END OF 2009-10 SEASON										
	G	GS	MPG	FG%	3P%	FT%	RPG	APG	SPG	BPG	PPG
LeBron	548	547	40.3	47.5	32.9	74.2	7.0	7.0	1.7	0.9	27.8
Carmelo	452	452	36.5	45.9	30.8	80.1	6.2	3.1	1.2	0.4	24.7

1) Look at the table. Which player averaged the most points per game (PPG)?

2) An assist is a pass that leads to a scored basket. Which player had the most assists (APG)?

3) If LeBron plays for 40.3 minutes per game (MPG) for four games, how many minutes does he play in total?

4) In five games LeBron gets the following number of rebounds:
   4 8 6 3 4
   What is his average RPG across the five games?

5) Carmelo attempts 50 free throws and makes 30 of them. What is his free throw percentage (FT%)?

LEBRON JAMES

In 2009, LeBron James starred in his own movie called "More Than A Game". The movie is about LeBron and his high school friends.

NBA team: Cleveland Cavaliers
Position: Forward
Date of birth: 30th December, 1984
Height: 2.03 m

CANDACE VS DIANA

CANDACE PARKER

3

The WNBA season only lasts for four months so Candace often plays in Russia during the winter.

WNBA team:
Los Angeles Sparks
Position: Forward
Date of birth: 19th April, 1986
Height: 1.93 m

Candace Parker and Diana Taurasi are two of the best female basketball players in the world. They both play in the WNBA and for the USA team. Candace and Diana play different positions and their style of play is very different. Compare their statistics and decide who you think comes out on top!

DIANA TAURASI

3

Diana's father, Mario, was a professional football player in Italy. He was a goalie – which might be why Diana is good with her hands!

WNBA team: Phoenix Mercury
Position: Guard
Date of birth: 11th June, 1982
Height: 1.83 m

COMPARE THE WNBA STARS QUIZ

Try these quiz questions about the WNBA stars.

1) Look at the information panels about Candace and Diana.
   a) Which is the older of the two players?
   b) Give the difference in height between the two players in centimetres.

2) In five seasons Candace makes the following average number of blocks per game (BPG):

   1.9   2.2   2.7   1.7   2.0

   a) Put the numbers in order starting with the smallest.
   b) What is the mean of Candace's average BPG across the five seasons?

The yellow table at the bottom of the page shows Candace Parker's and Diana Taurasi's statistics. Use the **Key To Statistics** box to find out what the numbers mean.

3) Which player had the highest percentage of 3 point shots (3P%)?

4) What percentage of her games did Diana start (GS)?

5) Candace made 51% of her field goals. If she attempted 200, how many did she miss?

WNBA CAREER STATISTICS TO THE END OF 2009

	G	GS	MPG	FG%	3P%	FT%	RPG	APG	SPG	BPG	PPG
Candace	58	57	33.2	51.0	32.0	74.0	9.6	3.1	1.0	2.2	16.2
Diana	198	198	32.6	44.0	37.0	83.0	4.5	4.0	1.3	1.0	20.3

THE HARLEM GLOBETROTTERS

The Harlem Globetrotters are the most famous team in basketball. They were formed in Chicago, USA, in 1926. The team began to clown around for their fans. Now they mix up amazing basketball skills with acrobatics, comedy acting and educational fun for their fans.

The Globetrotters and their mascot Globie have travelled to 120 countries.

The Globetrotters have played over 25,000 games. In February 2006, the team recorded its 22,000th win! In 2006, the team won 98.4% of its games.

GLOBETROTTERS QUIZ

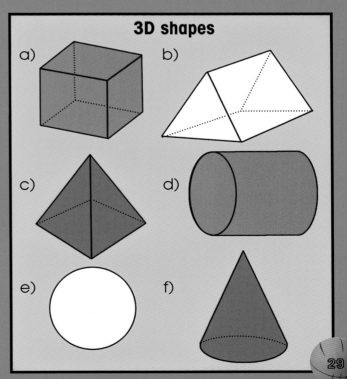

The Globetrotters have always been a brilliant team. Between 1971 and 1995, the team won 8829 games in a row!

Now try these quiz questions.

1) The Globetrotters had a winning streak of **8829 games**. Put these large numbers in order starting with the smallest.

   8892   8928   8829   8298   8289

2) The Globetrotters have played over 25,000 games.
   a) Divide 25,000 by 100
   b) Divide 25,000 by 10

3) Look at the **2D Shapes** below. Can you name them?

4) Look at the **3D Shapes** below. Can you name them?

5) How many faces does each 3D shape have?

2D shapes

a)

b)

c)

d)

e)

f)

3D shapes

a)

b)

c)

d)

e)

f)

9 BASKETBALL BASICS QUIZ

1 12 minutes
2 a) 12 b) 6 c) 15 d) 19 e) 8
3 5 seconds
4 86 m
5 1.14 m

11 RECORD BREAKERS QUIZ

1 Sun Mingming 236 cm
2 71 cm
3 1.89 m 1.98 m 2.01 m
  2.10 m 2.30 m
4 104
5 68

13 BASKETBALL HISTORY QUIZ

1 a) Bill Russell, 21,620
  b) Magic Johnson, 10,141
  c) Michael Jordan, 32,292
2 a) 9 tens b) 2 hundreds
  c) one thousand
3 George Mikan 400
  Bill Russell 1000
  Kareem Abdul-Jabbar 1600
  Magic Johnson 900
  Michael Jordan 1100
4 83
5 Michael Jordan

15 DREAM TEAM QUIZ

1 USA–Angola 68
  USA–Brazil 44
  USA–Croatia 33
  USA–Spain 41
  USA–Germany 43
  Quarter final
  USA–Puerto Rico 38
  Semi final
  USA–Lithuania 51
  Final
  USA–Croatia 32
2 Biggest difference = 68
  Smallest difference = 32

3 a) 120 b) 130 c) 100 d) 120
  e) 110 f) 120 g) 130 h) 120
4 938 points in total
  Mean score 117.25 points
5 a) $^1/_2$ b) $^1/_8$ c) $^1/_4$
  d) $^1/_{12}$ e) $^1/_5$

17 2008 USA OLYMPIC TEAM QUIZ

1 Odd – 101, 97, 119, 101
  Even – 92, 106, 116, 118
2 a) Germany
  b) China and Australia
  c) The final, USA–Spain
  11 points difference
3 a) 118 b) 119 c) 97 d) 116
4 515 points
5 The 1992 Dream Team
  earned the most points 938

19 WORLD CHAMPIONS QUIZ

1 a) Every four years
  b) 2014, 2018
2 1989, 2000
3 Japan
4 a) USA, Canada, Australia
  b) Five
5 Your diagram should look
  like this:

21 BIG LEAGUES QUIZ

1 LA Lakers won 50%
  Golden State won 90%
2 0.5; 0.25; 0.9; 0.6; 0.4
3 $^1/_2$ $^1/_4$ $^9/_{10}$ $^3/_5$ $^2/_5$
4 $^1/_4$ $^2/_5$ $^1/_2$ $^3/_5$ $^9/_{10}$
5 TEAM B 24 points
  TEAM C 37 games played
  TEAM D won 29 games
  TEAM E lost 10 games;
  51 points

23 YOU'RE THE COACH QUIZ

1 a) Carl b) $^{32}/_{40}$ or $^4/_5$
  c) 30 minutes d) 14 minutes
2 14 minutes   3 Combo C
4 a) Angle b; right angle
  b) Angle c
5 a) Angle e
  b) Angles a and d

25 COMPARE THE NBA STARS QUIZ

1 LeBron   2 LeBron
3 161.2 minutes   4 5
5 60%

27 COMPARE THE WNBA STARS QUIZ

1 a) Diana b) 10 cm
2 a) 1.7 1.9 2.0 2.2 2.7 b) 2.1
3 Diana
4 100%   5 98

29 GLOBETROTTERS QUIZ

1 8289 8298 8829 8892 8928
2 a) 250 b) 2500
3 a) Rhombus b) Kite
  c) Trapezium d) Parallelogram
  e) Hexagon
  f) Equilateral triangle
4 a) Cube b) Triangular prism
  c) Square based pyramid
  d) Cylinder e) Sphere f) Cone
5 a) 6 b) 5 c) 5 d) 3 e) 1 f) 2